W0009398

The Authority Guide to Marketing Your Business Book:

52 easy-to-follow tips from a book PR expert

by

Chantal Cooke

The Authority Guide to Marketing Your Business Book
52 easy-to-follow tips from a book PR expert
© Chantal Cooke

ISBN 978-1-909116-61-0
eISBN 978-1-909116-62-7

Published in 2016 by Authority Guides
authorityguides.co.uk

The right of Chantal Cooke to be identified as the author
of this work has been asserted by her in accordance with the
Copyright, Designs and Patents Act 1988.

A CIP record of this book is available from the British Library.

No responsibility for loss occasioned to any person acting or
refraining from action as a result of any material in this publication
can be accepted by the author or publisher.

Printed in the UK by TJ International, Padstow.

In loving memory of Roger M. Cooke and Muriel E. Cooke

Not all marketing people are writers, but all writers must learn to be marketers.

Joanne Kraft

Contents

Get a really good publishing partner, who really understands what's involved in publishing a business book. It seems like a relatively simple process – but it's not. And if you want sales, you need good PR. I would never do another book without having somebody who knows how to get it in front of people and get the reviews, get people talking about the book and getting it out in the media.

(Buist, 2009)

I made two mistakes with my first book: not working with a good publisher and not engaging a PR agent. With my next book I got it right – a great publisher [SRA Books] and a great PR [Chantal Cooke]. Within 20 months The Telegraph *had not only picked me up to be in the launch feature for their property club, but they also listed me as one of the top 25 most influential people in property. Chantal also got me coverage in* The Guardian, Observer, Daily Express, What Mortgage *and I got picked up by* Business Matters.

(Wusche, 2012)

Introduction

A book on the shelf is worth two in the box.

Macalister Stevens

Introduction

Writing a book is the easy bit. Marketing and selling it – that's the real challenge. Unfortunately for most business authors the great advice shared in their books ends up sitting in a box collecting dust. Sales may start well but it's not long before they are limping, and finally stopping altogether. Don't worry if this has happened to you – it's more common than you may think. And the good news: there are ways to give your book a brand new boost.

If you're still in the giddy stages of writing your book, then congratulations for thinking about the marketing early on – you can never start too early. And the earlier you do start, the more likely it is that your book will sell well and continue to sell.

The Authority Guide to Marketing Your Business Book will give you lots of ideas and advice on how to market your book – whether you're at the writing stage, your book is just about to be published or your book was published some time ago. Just as it's never too early to start, it's also never too late.

I am sure you put a lot of your energy and heart into writing your book (I know I did!), so don't hide it, get it out there so it can help those people and businesses that need to hear what you have to say.

If your author platform is not well built, you may lose readers to an inferior product that was simply easier to find because its platform was superior to yours.

Carole Jelen
literary agent

Building your
platform

'Build it, and they will come' only works
in the movies. Social Media is a 'build it,
nurture it, engage them and they may
come and stay.'

Seth Godin

Building your platform

You may have heard a lot about the author's 'platform' and how important this is. So what does this mean, why do you want one and how do you build one?

What is a platform?

It is your credibility (or authority) and your visibility within your target market. Simple as that.

Authority: Are you credible? Do you have authority as an author? What are your credentials? Have you had articles published in relevant publications? This is particularly important for business authors.

Visibility: Are you visible? Do people know about you? Do you have a 'fan' base or followers? Do you have a PR agent or a PR strategy? Have you had articles published in relevant publications? Where does your work regularly appear? How many people see it? What relevant communities are you a part of? Who do you influence? Are you regularly booked as a speaker? Do you have a social media presence?

Target market: Is your visibility relevant? Are you reaching your target market through your platform? For example, if your book is aimed at lawyers, but your authority and visibility is with dentists... your platform may not do you much good.

When should I start building my platform?

Start now. It is never too early or too late to start. Although it is true that the earlier you start, the better. In an ideal world you'd start building your platform as soon as you start thinking about writing the book.

It takes a long time to build a platform so start as soon as you can and do little and often rather than a big splurge and then nothing.

As a business person the chances are you already have some sort of platform; people already know you and you have a reputation within your industry. Use that and build upon it. Your platform will help sell the book, the book will help build your platform; every activity you do to market the book will help to sell more copies, build your platform and increase your business. And round and round it goes.

All the ideas in this book have been tried and tested and will help to market your book (and build your platform). So start as soon as you can and don't worry that you are too early or too late – just get started. Do as many activities as you can as often as you can. Don't fret about how much you do – just get started and do something. Everything helps and something is far better than nothing. Remember you don't need to be perfect – but you do need to get started.

Is your book ready to market?

A lot of times, people don't know what they want until you show it to them.

Steve Jobs

Is your book ready to market?

If your book has been traditionally published then it's pretty safe to say it's ready to be marketed. If you have self-published or worked with an independent publisher, then there are a few things you need to have in place before you can successfully start to market your book.

If you only intend to sell your book via your own website or at events, then you don't necessarily need the items below to be in place – just ensure your book has a great cover and looks high quality, and do be sure it's been proofed. Proofing errors will not do you, your book sales or your business any favours – in fact they will put many people off.

There are a number of items you must have in place if you wish to market your book as widely as possible and you also want to make it available to high street bookshops as well as digital bookstores (e.g. Amazon, Google Play, etc.).

One of these items is an International Standard Book Number (ISBN). Without an ISBN bookstores (of any kind) can't find and order your book.

Assuming your book has an ISBN it must also be registered with Nielsens (www.nielsenbookdata.co.uk).

It's important to ensure that your bibliographic data are accurate as they can be difficult to change later. This information is used by bookshops (online and high street) when choosing which books to order. The more information you can give the better. More information sells more books!

Bookshops order copies of books through wholesalers. So ensure your publisher has a distributor account with both wholesalers: Gardners and Bertrams. If your book is not in stock with them it will appear as 'out of stock' (i.e. unavailable) on Amazon and in bookshops.

Your book must also have a barcode. In order for bookshops (online and high street) to sell your book they need to be able to scan the barcode. This is a representation of your ISBN. It must be printed at the correct size and resolution.

Amazon is the market leader in terms of online book sales, but it's certainly not the only one. Make sure your book (both the physical and/or ebook version) is also listed with:

- Nook – from Barnes and Noble
- iBookstore – open an account and start selling your ebook
- Kobo – you upload your ebook onto their site, they sell your book, you get paid
- Waterstones.com – your publisher needs to register your book with Waterstones' Phoenix system. (This applies to both physical books and ebooks)
- iBooks Author – designed for authors of Multi-Touch textbooks for the iPad

- Scribd – once you are registered you can upload your ebook. Check out their FAQ to understand how you get paid for your work
- Payhip – you upload your ebook and start selling
- eBay – you can sell both physical and digital books on eBay

If you are registered with the wholesalers you will automatically be listed on these sites:

- WHSonline (www.whsmith.co.uk)
- The Book Depository (www.bookdepository.co.uk)
- Lovereading (www.lovereading.co.uk)
- Tesco (www.tesco.com/direct/books)
- Amazon (www.amazon.co.uk)

A full list with URLs can be found on The Book Booster membership website (www.TheBookBooster.com).

We all have our favourite online shops, so make it easy for people to purchase from theirs. By making your book available in as many places as possible you make it easier for people to find and easier for them to buy. There is no point putting lots of effort into marketing if people can't easily buy your book.

The best marketing doesn't feel like
marketing.

Tom Fishburne

Developing your strategy

Nothing great was ever achieved without enthusiasm.

Ralph Waldo Emerson

Developing your strategy

Before you start to market your book it's important to spend a few minutes thinking about what you want your book to achieve (for you and for your business). Once you are clear about that you can develop your marketing strategy. This doesn't need to be a huge document or take hours to develop – but it does need to be thought about, committed to paper and scheduled into your diary if you are to get the most from your book promotion activities.

In order to develop a strategy you have to ask yourself some questions – and give honest answers. In an ideal world you'd have unlimited time, money and resources to promote your book. But most of us don't live in this ideal world. So rather than trying to do everything, pick and choose the actions that most suit you.

Here are the areas you need to consider in order to develop your strategy.

What do I want to achieve by promoting my book?

This goes beyond the 'I want to sell some books' goal. Think broader. For example, I want more orders for my product or service; I'd like a publishing deal with a traditional publisher; I want more visitors to my website so I can create a sales funnel.

What you hope to achieve will influence which activities you choose and how much time and money you put into them.

Realistically how much time, energy and money can I put into this?

You need to be honest. Don't over commit yourself – whether that's in relation to time or money. Little and often is the trick to successful book promotion. Don't set yourself up to fail with impossible goals and the promise of unrealistic time commitments.

Which activities suit my personality and style?

Not every activity suits every book and every person. You will achieve far more if you play to your strengths rather than fight to overcome your 'weaknesses'. Choose the activities that make sense to you and appeal to you. If you enjoy something you are far more likely to do it. So choose activities you like.

Do I need external help and/or advice?

If there are areas you don't feel comfortable about tackling then consider getting external help. You don't need to do everything yourself or get someone else to do everything – you can outsource just the parts that you need help with.

Alternatively consider getting some coaching or training to help you with areas that you'd like to tackle yourself, but don't feel confident enough to start doing straight away.

Have I considered all the options?

Sometimes we can dismiss things we don't understand – so get a better understanding before you decide to ditch or commit to an activity.

How will I know if it's working?

Take a moment to think about where you and your book are now, where you want to be in six months, a year, etc. and what success will look like. Schedule regular reviews to check your progress and ensure you are still on course.

Am I being realistic?

By all means dream big – but be realistic about what is achievable and in what time frame. There is nothing more demotivating than huge impossible-seeming goals. Couple this with waking up each day knowing you haven't achieved that goal and you'll soon feel like giving up altogether.

Now that your book is ready to market, and you know what you want to achieve it's time to get started on proactively getting your book out to as many people as possible.

You can't expect to just write and have visitors come to you. That's too passive.

Anita Campbell

Tips

If you're not failing every now and again,
it's a sign you're not doing anything very
innovative.

Woody Allen

Tips

Here are 52 easy-to-follow tips to help you give your book a marketing boost.

1. Start using social media – it's invaluable for promoting your business book. Make sure you have accounts with Facebook, Twitter, LinkedIn and Google+. Others worth considering are Pinterest and Instagram (both are image-led).

   Facebook is good for gathering your 'fans' together, Twitter is good for making new connections, LinkedIn is a must for every businessperson, and although Google+ is not yet anywhere near as big as Twitter and Facebook, it is still a useful social network for the business author. It allows you to sort your connections into 'circles', for example, friends, clients, business associates, etc. Unlike other social networks this means you can post targeted updates to specific circles. Google+ also boosts your visibility in the Google search engine.

   Keep all your social media posts relevant and interesting. And use pictures to attract attention. Social media posts with photos, rich links and videos get more attention. Images and videos are also easy to share, extending your reach. So get snapping! For example, photos of your book launch, a book signing, fans with your book, your book on display in a bookshop, you writing or giving a speech, something funny (and relevant) that you've noticed, industry news that potential readers of your book would also be interested in – anything that helps people connect with you by building your credibility and visibility.

Other ideas include: posting a draft of a chapter asking for feedback; publicising book tour dates; your latest blog post; great reviews of your book. Or how about uploading a free chapter – to entice new readers?

2 Create a series of top tips from the content in your book and post these once a week on your social media profiles, say they are taken from your book and add a link to your book on Amazon. This will showcase your expertise, build your authority and visibility, and let people know the value they will get from buying your book.

3 Set up a Facebook Page. There is a difference between Facebook profiles and Facebook Pages. According to Facebook rules, your profile should be for you and your friends on a personal level. Your Page is for the public front of you, that is, the author or business owner.

If you don't already have a Facebook Page, then set one up and use it to promote your book (and your business). Invite your friends, and also add a social sharing button to your website. This is the blue 'f' you often see on the top right of websites – when you click it, it will either take you direct to the Facebook Page or it will allow you to 'like' the Facebook Page. Make it as easy as possible for people to 'like' your Page. Once they have liked it they will get updates from your Page in their timeline. Your Page allows you to market to people who already like you. People who like your Page are already interested in you and what you're doing next – so keep them informed.

Note: if they want to continue to receive updates from your Page, they have to keep 'liking' and/or replying to your posts. In order to ensure they do this, you need to keep the posts interesting and engaging!

Ask your fans to 'comment' on and 'like' your posts and, better still, to 'share' your posts (these options appear just underneath the post).

To create a Page, click 'Create Page' in the left-hand column on your Facebook profile.

4 Set up or join a Facebook or LinkedIn Group. Groups are a bit like forums. They exist in both Facebook and LinkedIn. They gather together like-minded people. The best way to use groups is to join other peoples'. Find groups that contain your target readership, join them and start interacting with the members. Don't sell to them (no one likes a hard sell or being confronted with relentless promotion), instead share your knowledge, offer advice, answer or ask questions, share useful information (if it's not your own then be sure to credit the author) and recommend other great business books you have read. All of these activities will build your platform (visibility and authority).

Facebook: to find a Group click 'Groups' in the left-hand column on your Facebook profile.

LinkedIn: to find a Group click 'Interests' in the top menu, and then click on 'Groups'.

5 Advertise your events on Facebook. You can create event notifications for your Page or Group to spread the word

about events you're holding, for example, your book launch, a talk you are giving or a book signing. Even if you aren't the organiser, you can still create and promote the event via Facebook.

You can also use this as a way to find useful events for networking and promoting your book, for example, business networking meetings, author meet-ups or talks that might attract your target audience.

To create an event, click 'Create Event' in the left-hand column on your Facebook profile. From here, you can customise the event, edit its privacy settings and invite guests. You must include an event name and time.

6. Start tweeting and using #hashtags – these are great ways to reach new people. Your tweets (in fact all your updates on any social media platform) should give an insight into your personality, be relevant to your book, be entertaining, be informative, be funny or be interesting. In other words, be worth reading and, at least sometimes, be worth retweeting.

The idea is to let people get to know you and what you write about. So tell people about you and your book. Also reply to other people's tweets and engage other people in conversation.

Use hashtags to help people find you and your book. These are searchable keywords within a tweet, Facebook or Google+ update (although they are used far more frequently on Twitter). Hashtags are created by adding the # symbol before any word or series of words (no spaces between the words). Anyone can create a #hashtag – there is no set list.

Hashtags are a good way to find conversations that may be of interest/relevant to you. For example, search for #businessquestion or #boostingprofit. See what people are talking about. If any look interesting or relevant to you, follow those people and reply, like, share or retweet (RT).

Replying starts a conversation. Retweeting gives your followers additional interesting content and helps you to make friends with the people you are retweeting.

If someone RTs one of your tweets – thank them.

Also add #hashtags to your own tweets to let people find your tweets by topic. For example, #businessadvice, #increasesales, #HRadvice. Think in terms of what your target audience might search for.

By searching for specific #hashtags within Twitter you can see which ones are popular. At www.hashtags.org you can type in a #hashtag and the site will show you a graph of the previous 24 hours' activity. By looking at what's popular right now (i.e. trending) you can think about ways to make the social media updates about your book relevant to that trend.

7　If you enjoy social media (and not everyone does!) then check out other social networking sites. For example, Ning (create your own social network), Ryze (for business people), MySpace (17–25-year-old audience), BranchOut (App on Facebook often used for recruitment), Plaxo (online address book), Shelfari (social cataloguing site for books) and weRead (online community of book enthusiasts). Also check out social bookmarking sites like StumbleUpon, Digg, Delicious, Reddit, Slashdot, BuzzFeed, etc.

Sign up to Goodreads.com This is a social cataloguing website where readers can create their own book lists, post reviews, give suggestions, discuss books, etc. If your book is on Amazon it will also be listed on Goodreads (as the website is now owned by Amazon).

(8) Consider spending a few pounds on Facebook Adverts. These are quick and easy to set up and you can cap your spend at, say, £3 per day. Adverts are highly targeted – if you have a good profile of your target reader, you can be ridiculously choosy about who sees your ad. For example, you can target for location, language, education, work, age, gender, birthday, relationship status, interests, connections and friends of connections. You can even ask the ad to avoid people who have already 'liked' your Page.

You can promote individual posts, drive visitors to your website, generate Page 'likes', even offer a discount code for your book.

To create a Facebook Advert go to www.facebook.com/ads/create and from there you will be guided through a three-step process for creating your ads.

Facebook Pages have good in-built analytics, which can give you insights into the number of likes, comments and shares each of your posts has received.

Analytics help you gauge what's working and what attracts people, so that you can tweak your approach.

Only admins/managers of a Page can see this information. It's hidden from everyone else.

(9) Get noticed by your target audience within Twitter by using @Mentions, replies and retweeting. An @Mention is a way of referencing another person within a tweet so that they

are aware you are talking about them. You do this by typing the symbol @ and then the person's Twitter name.

Using an @Mention means the person you're talking about receives notification that you've mentioned them. Talking to and about people this way means you can have conversations and build relationships; it increases the likelihood of those people reading/responding to/sharing your tweets.

When using @Mentions you need to do so using their correct Twitter name. This may not be the same as their real name. Twitter names always have the @ symbol at the front.

If you want a particular person to notice you, then @Mention them, or reply to one of their tweets or RT their content. Retweeting gives your followers new content, spreads the love around (so hopefully others will RT you – putting you in front of their followers) and gets you noticed by the person whose content you have retweeted.

10 Host a 'Hangout' in Google+. It is one of the most popular features of Google+.

A Hangout is basically a group video chat that is both super simple and free. You can include up to ten people at a time in a Hangout party.

For example, you could hold a reading – with people all over the world. Or connect with a book club and host a chat just for them. Arrange a Q&A session linked to your book or do a mini workshop for potential customers and offer them a discount if they buy your book at the end.

If you want to reach more than ten people, then have a Hangout On Air, which allows you to stream your video on both Google+ and YouTube. People can watch it on either platform, and Google+ records the video and sends it to you via email.

Learn more about Hangouts at
https://hangouts.google.com/

11 Do more with LinkedIn. As a business person you are probably already using LinkedIn – so make sure your connections know about your book. Post updates about the book, tips from the book or special offers. Interact within relevant LinkedIn Groups (i.e. those that gather together your target audience), and use 'Advanced' search (top right hand corner of the search box) to seek out industry professionals who might be interested in your book; engaging you for a talk, reading or signing; or working with you as an affiliate to sell your book, and gain introductions to them from people you already know.

Advanced search allows you to search by keywords, job title, industry, location, the company they currently or have previously worked for, etc. The search results will also indicate how closely you are connected to them in your existing network – so you can start with people with whom you already have a connection.

You can also display samples of your work on your LinkedIn profile. These are called 'work samples'. This is an opportunity to display an extract from your book, the front cover, the back cover blurb, or even a selection of reviews.

See
http://help.linkedin.com/app/answers/detail/a_id/34325

12 Google+ has a very useful feature called Search plus Your World – this means that anyone who has you in their Circles will see your results high up in any Google.com search they perform. It's this combination of both social and search engine optimisation (SEO) that makes Google+ a social network worth engaging with.

So as an author make sure to add the people you'd like to reach (e.g. publisher, agents, influential book reviewers, business journalists, etc.) to your Circles. In all likelihood, many of them will reciprocate by adding you to their Circles. This means they will start to see your posts, not only in Google+, but also in Google.com when they're searching.

You can add a personal touch to those search results by ensuring your photo appears next to your website and Google+ post links. You simply connect your Google+ account with the home page of your website. This single action tells Google+ you're a real person so they (Google) will begin displaying your photo next to your search results.

13 Google+ also has Business Pages (a bit like Facebook Pages). Google+ considers all business to be local. This can be an opportunity for business authors as well. People (readers, shops, reading groups, etc.) like a local connection, so your Page can help you to make those local connections.

Another advantage of a Google+ local business Page is that Google serves up those results first when anyone does a local search. In other words you'll appear in Google+ and in Google searches.

Once you've set up your Page you can use Google+ as yourself or as your Page (again, similar to Facebook).

You might choose to create an author Page, and/or a Page for each book. The choice is yours – you can have more than one Page. If you don't want your Page to be local, then you can set up a Page for a brand. This removes the geographical location link.

People (readers) can post reviews on your Page, and these will show up in the Google search results – putting them right in front of anyone doing a relevant search.

Remember to include a good quality photo; post regular updates; #hashtag keywords and topics to help people find/search specific topics; mix some fun, personal updates (that show you are a real human being!) with your 'promotional' updates; and keep it interesting and relevant to your audience.

14 Take photos – and post them on Pinterest and Instagram.

Pinterest is essentially a photo sharing website. Think of it as a pin board full of photos on a particular theme. A 'board' is where the user's pins are located. Users can have multiple boards. A 'pin' is an image that has either been uploaded or linked from a website onto a board.

Other users can re-pin your pins, meaning they can pin your image to their board as well. Users can also browse, comment and like other pins. (Just like Facebook: imagine you've posted a photo on Facebook – now people can like it, comment on it or share it.)

Instagram is an online photo/video sharing and social networking service that enables users to take pictures and videos, and share them on a variety of social networking platforms, including Facebook and Twitter. The maximum duration for an Instagram video is 15 seconds.

Pinterest and Instagram are especially useful if your book is visually led – photography, art, cookery, design, crafts, etc. But if you love taking photos or like thinking visually then these two sites can be useful promotional tools.

For example, if you're the author of a cookery book, create a Pinterest board of 'my favourite cakes'; an architect – 'best modern architecture in the UK'; a business advice book – 'business books that have changed my life' or 'great business book covers that made me want to buy the book'; an art expert, auctioneer, gallery owner, museum curator, interior designer – 'up and coming artists to look out for'; an accountant – 'bank notes from around the world'.

And while you are out and about take snaps of items relevant to your book: cookery book – pictures of great food or food that's beautifully presented; jewellery designer – fabulous jewellery, items in nature that inspire your jewellery; web designer – great home pages, attractive branding, clever ways people have promoted their website; and of course pictures of your book in various places.

15 Build a database of people interested in your book – and do this as soon (i.e. as early) as possible. Encourage people to sign up for more information: ask them via your social media; offer them a free gift (for example, a free ebook; see tip 43); have a sign-up box on your website; run competitions online, at events and exhibitions; email friends, clients, suppliers and ask if they'd be interested to know more about your book and if it's OK for you to add them to the mailing list.

Ideally, a month or so before publication email all your contacts and tell them about the book and give them the opportunity to pre-order copies via your website. Also promote the pre-order opportunity on all your social media, your website, your email signature, etc.

Don't just email once – keep them up to date and email them about once a week or so for the month prior to publication. Keep it short and friendly, respect unsubscribe requests and don't keep emailing people who have already bought the book.

People like the idea of being the first, of getting something before everyone else, so give them the opportunity to pre-order your book and be among the very first people to receive it – hot off the presses!

If your book has already been published, don't worry. Still work on building that database and still use it to promote and sell your book. A list of 'warm' leads of people interested in your book is an invaluable marketing tool.

16 Start a blog, or if you have one already then make sure it's kept up to date and has a sidebar where people can easily buy your book. If you're driving traffic to your blog, use the opportunity to sell your book. Make it easy for visitors to click and buy.

Keep the blog relevant to your book and don't use it purely as a sales tool – you'll put people off. Give them useful, interesting content that keeps them coming back.

For example:

- Comment on relevant news items
- Offer tips to your readers
- Write a critique (e.g. if you are a graphic designer perhaps you can talk about what works or not in some of the most famous brand logos)
- Blog about some of the areas you'd like to have included in your book but didn't have space for
- Update your readers on your latest news
- Share new developments in your sector

- Write about new discoveries or research relevant to your topic

- Tell them about activities you are involved in that are relevant to your book, including lectures, book signings, etc. You can write about these before, during and after the events

- Interview other people, perhaps other writers or experts, with a relevance to your book's audience

- Invite fellow experts to write a blog post for you and offer your expertise to other complementary (non-competitive) blogs

Give your blog, video, podcast a great headline. This doesn't necessarily mean a clever or obscure headline. Often a 'do what it says on the tin' headline is best. If it's too obscure, people don't understand what they are going to get or why they should take the time to engage with it, and more often than not they won't bother to find out.

Use different headlines for the same blog depending on where you are promoting it. On your own blog page you can be a little 'cleverer' with the headline. On external sites where people have not yet necessarily 'bought into you', be clearer. As appropriate adapt the content on your headline to suit the place where you are posting it.

17 Creating short videos can really help to sell your book. These can be included on your blog (don't make every post a video – some people like to read or listen), on your website and in your social media posts. It's a good idea to create your own YouTube channel (YouTube is now the second biggest search engine) and post all your videos there. Also consider hosting a Google+ Hangout (see tip 10).

Keep your videos short, under four minutes preferably. If you have more to say, break it up into a video series.

Your video content can be: tips; how to; latest news; someone interviewing you about your book; you interviewing other business authors; a short extract from your book; an explanation of the implications of new industry legislation; interviewing a successful case study; reviews/testimonials for your book; etc.

Whatever and however you choose to use video, think first about the audience. They are the most important people when creating a video.

18 More and more people have MP3 players and iPods and listen to podcasts while commuting or in the car. Be mindful of the sound quality – people are often listening in noisy environments and poor sound quality can make hearing the content a real challenge. Keep audio short and pacey, don't add music unless it really adds to the podcast and even then ensure that the music is copyright free (no, you can't use your favourite pop song).

The ideas for video (see tip 17) can also work for audio. You have the added advantage that you don't need to be in the same room as a person you are interviewing – so this is a chance to look further afield and go global.

What do you want your audience to know or do as a result of your blog, video or podcast? If you can tell them things they didn't know or give them perspectives that they didn't have, then they will keep coming back for more. But they may also want to know what to do, so it's worth considering if you have an 'ask' of your readers. But don't sell, sell, sell or constantly push them to your book – strike a balance.

Load all your podcasts onto your website, promote them in your blog and on social media and create an RSS feed so people can get an alert when a new podcast is uploaded. Put a link to your podcasts in your email signature.

19 Promote your blog, videos and audio. All of these are promoting your book, so make sure you tell people about them. The same techniques you use to promote your blog, video or audio can also be used to promote your book directly. However, if the promotions are always about the book, then they can become 'wallpaper' and people don't notice them. So by changing the content you keep the message new, fresh and visible:

- Use social media to promote your blog. Link your blog into Facebook, Twitter, LinkedIn, etc.

- Add a www.stumbleupon.com badge to your blog to make it easy for people to share

- Add your blog, video and audio URLs to your email signature

- Post links to relevant blog posts in forums (only when relevant and adding value – don't spam)

- Encourage other bloggers you know to link to you, and return the favour

- Swap blog articles with fellow bloggers

- Email your contacts and tell them about your blog. Remember to provide a link

- Tell people – I mean speak to them!

- Add your blog to your business cards – and hand them out

- If you have a blog you want a particular person to read – email them a link

- Ask your contacts to tell their contacts

Set up an RSS feed. RSS or 'Really Simple Syndication' allows people to subscribe to your blog and get your blog posts sent to them at their feed reader – rather than having to go looking for them.

Many popular news sites and blogs provide an RSS feed, which you can subscribe to. All you need is a feed reader to view its contents.

This is a great way to drive more traffic to your blog. Instead of relying on people to bookmark your site and return regularly, their RSS reader keeps your site fresh in their minds.

RSS feeds also prevent updates from you being caught by email spam filters; rather than sending a newsletter, which often gets caught in the spam filter or ends up being deleted along with hundreds of other newsletters, the RSS feed bypasses all of this. So although that doesn't mean newsletters are dead, it does mean that you should also consider an RSS feed – you want to be able to reach as many people as possible, and you want to make it as easy as possible for them to hear from you.

Go on a blog tour. Put simply, a blog tour is you/your book being featured on a number of blogs, on different dates – as though you were on tour.

Exactly how you are featured on each blog will depend on the requirements of the blog. It could be a book review, Q&A, an extract from the book, a book giveaway or any other idea that suits the blogger's style and audience.

New blogs are appearing and disappearing all the time, so you'll need to hunt around on Google for the ones that are appropriate for your book. Write an individual pitch for each blog. Don't do a mass mailing. Write to the blog owner and explain who you are, briefly what your book is about and ask them if they'd like a contribution from you as you'd love to 'stop' at their blog on your tour.

You'll need to promote the tour yourself – part of the attraction of being part of your tour is that you'll promote their blog as well. So make sure you have all their social media details.

The key to a successful blog tour is to understand the blogs you are 'stopping' at and provide them with interesting, engaging information.

22 Invite fellow authors to write a guest blog on your blog; they will attract new readers and promote their contribution to their followers. Offer to write for other (relevant) blogs. Share the blogging love and everyone will benefit.

23 Add your details to Amazon's Author Central. When readers find a book interesting, they look for more information about the author. On Amazon this information comes from your profile in their Author Central section. You can use this to give readers more information about yourself, any other books you have written, and any events/workshops, etc. you have planned. Make sure you keep this up to date – if readers are going to your profile it's because they want to know more about you and your books, so don't disappoint them, and don't waste the opportunity.

24 Enrol your Kindle ebook in Amazon's Kindle Direct Publishing (KDP) Select and make the most of the ability to offer the book for free for five days in every three months. This may seem counter-intuitive but you need lots of reviews and a good ranking to make your book fly on Amazon, and giving away a few copies for free can really help. (Note: According to Amazon's Terms and Conditions an author can only take part in the KDP ebook offers – changing the price, etc. – if the ebook is only uploaded to Amazon. It cannot be uploaded to any other platform.)

Before you do this it's best to have at least four or five good reviews for your book already posted on Amazon. Books with a few five star reviews do far better than those with none – and since you're giving the book away for free, you want to get as much out of it as you can.

Schedule your free giveaway at least a month in advance so you have plenty of time to promote it. I'd suggest scheduling two consecutive free days to start with. Friday and Saturday can be good as you catch both those who surf at work and those who surf at home.

Now that you have your dates, it's time to tell everyone. There are a lot of websites, Facebook Pages and Twitter feeds that advertise free books – so let them know about yours. Many of them need at least one month's notice. Most are free but a few are paid for.

You can find a list of the websites, Facebook Pages and Groups, and Twitter feeds at TheBookBooster.com (This is a membership site. To join use promo AG2MYBB.)

Submit your books to the websites at least a month before the promotion.

Also be sure to tell all your contacts by adding a link on your website, telling your social media followers and including a link in your email signature.

Once the free promotion is live, log into your KDP Select account and add new tags, for example, Kindle freebie, free ebook, Kindle free, to your book page.

Next turn your attention to social media. Tweet about your free book and include @Mentions of Twitter users who promote free books. Be sure to include a link to the Amazon page for your free Kindle book. Post messages about your free book, with a link to its Amazon page, on the free Kindle book Facebook Pages and Groups.

After the free promotion on Amazon has ended, continue to keep an eye on your sales. As your sales dwindle, drop the price. If this kick-starts your sales, push the price up a little. As they start to slow, drop it down again. This can sometimes give your book a real boost.

Eventually, however, your book will (in 99 per cent of cases) drop down the rankings. So start thinking about your next free promotion. Ideally leave about two months between each promotion – any earlier than that and you'll be reaching the same people.

Don't be put off by the idea of giving your book away for free – it's a great way to reach new readers and boost sales of your book after the free period. If you've written more than one book, then giving one away for free can have a big, and positive, impact on your other titles.

25 Play with the price of the ebook version of your book. On platforms like Amazon and other sites where you can control the price, play around. It's not always the lower price that generates the most sales. Higher prices give a perceived sense of quality. A reduction from a high price is more attractive than a constant low price. Test what works, keep track of what you did and what impact this had on sales. And if you're selling on more than one platform, vary it across platforms. It's amazing what a difference the price can make to your book sales.

26 If you get any reviews that aren't on Amazon, ask the reviewer if they would be willing to post their review on Amazon. Some will be willing to do so – and every single positive review helps the sales of your book.

Ask your reviewer for permission to post their review on your blog, website, newsletter, etc. Include quotes from the review on some of your promotional material.

Send copies of your best reviews to bookshops – especially those local to you.

27 List your book for sale on Amazon Marketplace (www.amazon.co.uk/gp/seller/sell-your-stuff.html). You can do this regardless of whether or not it's registered with the wholesalers. You choose the price, Amazon takes the money and pays this over to you (minus a commission) on a monthly basis, and you pack and post the book to the buyer. You can also offer extras like signed copies.

28 Promote your book in your newsletter and sometimes include a discount code to tempt the 'undecideds'.

Ask business colleagues and friends if they'd be willing to add a few words about your book to their newsletter and include a link so people can purchase the book easily and quickly. If you are able to offer their readers a discount code, this can work as an incentive to encourage your colleagues and friends to promote you; they look good for having negotiated the discount, and if their readers think they might get a good deal by opening the newsletter, they are more likely to do so.

29 Be a reverse thief. Many places have free bookshelves where you can pick up a second-hand book for free. The idea being that once you've finished the book you'll put it back on this shelf or another free shelf elsewhere so that other people can enjoy the book. You often find them at train and underground stations, or in coffee shops. Grab a few copies of your book and every time you pass a free shelf, donate a copy.

You can also pop into a few independent bookshops and pop a copy of your book on the relevant shelf in the store. As long as the book has a barcode and ISBN number the shop can put it through the till if someone picks it up and decides to buy it. If the bookshop sees that the book is selling, they will order more copies and stock it on their shelves.

30 Add a link to your book on Amazon (or your chosen retailer) to your email signature. Sometimes add a 'discount code' as well – but give it an expiry date. And don't do it too often – you want to make people think there is a time limit and a scarcity value. It's easy to add a discount (or promotional) code to your books when you are selling them via your Amazon Marketplace account. Search for 'understanding promotions' within the 'help' section of Amazon.

31 Make sure your website (or other relevant contact details) are in the book so people can buy more books, book you for a talk or signing, buy your services, etc. Give them more information about you and what you offer at the back of the book. If they have got that far, the chances are they want more, so tell them how to get it. If you've forgotten to include your contact details in your book, then get some attractive bookmarks printed with your details on them and give one away with every book.

32 Hold a launch event. For starters you deserve to celebrate – you're now a published author. But it's also a good excuse to get business colleagues, associates and clients (past, present and future) together, remind them what you do and encourage them to buy a copy. Most people expect to buy a copy of the book at the launch – so you won't need to (and shouldn't anyway) do a hard sell.

If you are using a book as a form of business card, then you may decide to give everyone who attends the launch a free copy. This means you can do a bit more of a sell on your services on the night, although a hard sell is never a good idea (even if they are getting a free book). You can also ask them all to review the book for you – do it gently and say there is no obligation to do so, but you'd really appreciate it. Most won't ever get round to it, but a few will – and that's a great start.

Launch events are also a good excuse to invite journalists. Most won't attend but the event may encourage a few to write about you or interview you about your book.

33 Hold your launch event in a bookshop. Many independent bookshops, and also Waterstones stores, will be willing to host your event. You'll need to supply the wine and nibbles and bring the crowd, but they will provide the venue for free and handle sales on the night.

Usually you'll give them a number of books, they will sell these and put them through their tills and handle all the money while you schmooze your guests. At the end of the night they will tell you how many copies they have sold and give you back any unsold ones. They will then ask you to invoice them for the books they've sold at the usual trade price.

In addition, they will often buy a few more copies to put on their shelves – something that can be extremely valuable, and something that you should shout about on your website and on social media.

Remember to get a photographer for the event – and use the pictures on your social media, your website, in your newsletter and on your Amazon Author Central page (where you can add up to eight photos). Get some pictures of you signing copies in front of the bookshop's signage or logo as this will add weight to the credibility of your book.

34 Anywhere that your book is for sale, including the bookshop where you did your launch, pop in and photograph the book on the shelf, then post a picture on all your social media accounts identifying the shop. Use @Mentions, tag them on Facebook, post on their Facebook Page and anywhere else you can help to promote them and your book – ideally where they will see it too!

35 Send press releases about the publication and launch of the book to your local media and relevant business media. Offer to send a review copy and make sure they know you are available for interview and have your contact details. If you are contacting the local press be sure to emphasise that you are local.

36 PR is an excellent marketing tool for a business book as it works on many levels. It promotes the book, you as an expert and your business – all in one go. It also builds your platform, drives visitors to your site, boosts your SEO and helps you to dominate Google in your niche. The key is to keep the PR going long after the book's publication.

You can do this by writing advice-based articles inspired by, or developed from, the content of your book. By writing for your target audience and providing them with useful, relevant information, journalists will be more likely to publish your content and credit you and your book.

If you are doing any other PR activity, then be sure to mention that you are the author of [your book title]. Every mention of your book builds your profile, your authority and awareness of your book.

PR takes a lot of time, but it is absolutely possible to do it yourself, if you're willing to do the legwork. Alternatively, consider hiring an expert. A good PR agent should have lots of ideas about how to keep the media coverage rolling in long after the initial publication.

For more advice on how to do your own PR check out my other book, *PR Demystified: How to get free publicity by giving journalists what they really need*.

37 Take your book with you everywhere. Always have a copy with you, so you can show it to people, sell them a copy there and then, pose with it in photos, etc. You never know when you'll meet a potential reader, or when your book might tip the balance when it comes to closing a deal.

Wherever appropriate, if you are being photographed, make sure you're holding a copy of your book.

38 Have some attractive postcards, business cards or bookmarks printed with details of your book, a picture of the cover, how to buy it, and your website, email and social media details. Again, you never know when you might meet a potential reader – and cards are easier to carry than a bag full of books. Leave enough space to be able to hand write a discount code on the card. As you are giving them the card, add the code and tell them this is specially for them and if they buy the book from your website, quoting this code within the next x days, they will get x per cent off. This can help focus their mind and get them to act quickly. And they will be grateful to you for giving them a good deal.

39 If you are speaking at an event make a point of mentioning your book and telling the audience that they can buy a copy from you after your talk. Don't make it a vague embarrassed throwaway at the end. Tell them clearly you have a book, tell them very briefly what it's about and what they'll get by reading it, hold up a copy to show them, and then tell them you'll be selling copies later. Tell them when and where so it's really easy for them to buy from you. People find lots of excuses not to do things, even things they want to do, so any hurdle, even if it's just not knowing where to find you after the talk, is a barrier to a sale. So make sure you pull down all the barriers.

40 Promote your book on your exhibition stands. If you are already attending exhibitions on behalf of your business, then use the opportunity to sell your book. It's a talking point for your stand, and if your business is based around services rather than products, then a book can give you something tangible on your stand with which to engage people.

You'll be meeting dozens of potential readers and a book is the perfect low priced, low risk way to get to know you without committing to a large spend. We all know leaflets and brochures end up in the recycling within a few days of attending an exhibition, but a book will stick around and be remembered and will keep you in their mind.

41 If you don't have the resources to have your own exhibition stand, then team up with fellow business authors and share a stand where you can all work together to sell your books (and of course your services). You can also offer all the books as a bundle at a special price, or throw in a free gift. By working together you can cross-promote each other's books and reach new people. You can also share the burden of staffing the stand.

42 Speak to your local independent bookshop – many of them like to support local authors. Ask if they will stock your book or perhaps put a display in their window and mention that you are local. Offer to do a signing, or an evening talk or workshop. Listen carefully to what works best for them – they know their audience so be willing to be flexible and adapt to their needs. Always promote anything they do for you (press releases, social media, your website, etc.) as most small, independent bookshops are struggling, so any help you can give them to get people through their doors will win you brownie points. And having their support can make a huge difference to the sales of your book.

43 Write a short ebook that complements your main book. Make sure it is proofed and edited properly and offers advice that is useful and relevant to the readers you are targeting with your main book. Include details of your book, what the readers will get if they read it (i.e. the benefits) and how to buy it. Give the ebook away for free (see tip 24), or for a very low price, on Amazon, on your website, via your social media, to your contacts, etc. The ebook is your way of showing them the value they will get from buying your book – so make sure you give them something valuable in the ebook (not just a sales pitch).

44 If your book is suitable, write to all the colleges and universities running courses related to your book's content and ask them if they would include it on their reading lists. Send them quotes from a few of your best reviews and explain what the book covers and how it could help their students. Offer to send them a copy so they can check it out. This takes a bit of work but can ultimately lead to a lot of sales, year after year.

45 Make sure you have a website (as a business person I am sure you do), that your book is displayed prominently on it and is easy to buy, either direct from the site or by clicking on a link to Amazon, etc.

Also consider having a specific website (which may be just a single page) that tells people about the book, what they will get if they read it, how they can buy it, etc. and optimise this page for Google. Get a PayPal (or similar) plug-in so people can buy your book there and then. If you are going to buy Google or Facebook Adverts, then this is the page to direct people to. You want them to buy the book – don't let them get distracted by everything else.

46 Get as many reviews as possible. Good reviews, especially on Amazon, but elsewhere as well, will really help to sell your book.

Contact reviewers in the business press (online and elsewhere); approach bloggers who blog about business or your industry; put out a call on social media for people who would be willing to review your book on Amazon (or elsewhere) in return for a free copy (you will get a few freeloaders, so choose your reviewers carefully); look for reviewers on Amazon who have positively reviewed books in your sector, click on their username by the review and it will often give you their email address, email and offer them a copy of your book and ask for a review; whenever you sell a book ask politely if the buyer would consider posting a review once they have read it; if you attend a regular business networking group ask your fellow members if they would be willing to post a review in return for a copy; and, of course, ask your friends, family and business associates if they'd be willing to post a review.

47 Take your book with you when you go networking and make a point of attending new networking groups in order to promote your book to new, potential readers. Take a few copies, plus your 'book business cards' (see tip 38), and rather than pitch your business, pitch your book. I know you want to attract new clients so it's tempting to want to pitch the business, but talking about the book positions you as an expert, showcases your business (after all the book is based on your business expertise) and gives you credibility by letting people know you are a published author. Quite a few people will buy your book there and then – and that means they will remember you and you'll be sitting on their shelf/desk weeks after you met them.

48 Use your book as a business card. No you don't want to give a copy to everyone you meet while networking, but if there is someone you'd really like to impress and make a stronger connection with, then give them a free copy of your book. They will remember you, and be more likely to refer you after reading the book, even if they themselves have not used your services. Also, everyone likes a free gift – and most people feel as though they ought to give something back in return, so these people are more likely to recommend you and/or your book, to tell people about your book on social media and to post a review.

49 Run a competition and offer a few copies of your book as a prize. This is another excuse to tell people about your book and it allows you to collect their email addresses or the business cards (for example, if you are at an event) of people who are interested in you and your book. Announce the winners publicly (on your website, social media, etc.) and email the other people saying you are sorry they didn't win, but you'd like to offer them a discount if they buy your book. You can now market your book and your business to these people. But don't spam them, don't overload them with emails, keep the emails relevant and useful (not just sales messages) and give them an easy way to unsubscribe (and respect this).

50 Share the love. Promote other authors, and congratulate them and commiserate with them. Do this verbally, on your blog, via social media, in your newsletter – wherever it is relevant. Authors tend to help each other as they all know how hard it is to market and sell their books, so if you support them, they are very likely to support you in return.

51 Offer to give some of your best clients or suppliers a number of your books for free so that they can use them as gifts/giveaways for their clients. It helps you to build the relationship with them, and they will market your book for you by giving out copies and telling everyone how generous they are and how great you are. It's a win–win.

52 Affiliate programmes/sites like ClickBank and Tradebit can help you to market the digital version of your book as they offer an online marketplace for digital information products. The sites work as a way of connecting content creators (you, with your book) and marketers who will market and sell your digital book in return for an affiliate fee (a commission). You often need to give them 50 per cent of the cover price, but they do all the legwork – so this is an avenue that's worth exploring.

Many a small thing has been made large
by the right kind of advertising.

Mark Twain

Case study 1

Increasingly, the mass market is turning into a mass of niches.

Chris Anderson
author of *The Long Tail*

Case study 1

Andrew Jenkins is author of *You Are More Than You Think*. Here he talks about how he sold around £1,000 worth of his books before it was even published.

I like to plan for success, so asked myself, 'How do I get this book out of my garage?' And it became a key motivator for me, not having a whole pile of books left in my garage. Today I've only got a few boxes left; we've sold about 70 per cent of those books so far, which is pretty good!

I decided to build a database of people that I could contact to tell them about my book. I like processes and so I started slowly to build a list. I found it quite hard at first. I built this list from LinkedIn, Facebook and the people that I know. So when the time came I had a database ready and I put that into MailChimp, so I got ready to advertise to them at the right point.

I realised that the big mountain of actually writing the book was just a little hill. And the real big mountain is: how the hell am I going to sell it? The real rubber meets the road when you've got the book in your hands and you've got to sell the damn thing!

So the next job was to get a website – I think that's really important for every business author. I had a gut feeling that this could be a good channel so I spent a little bit more money for a PayPal plug-in for the website to sell the book. That way I get more profit if I sell it through the website and I can sell signed copies.

In terms of pre-sales it hadn't actually occurred to me to do pre-sales originally, but people do it all the time, so I went for it, the book was published in May, and the website went live 1st of March. By then I already had a database of people and a website and the ability to sell books through pre-order. So we put some wording on the website to sell the book and I used my database of contacts from LinkedIn and Facebook and my clients and sent out personal emails and said, 'Look, I'm really excited about publishing this book, have a look at the website and if you're interested you can pre-order.' And do you know what, those people bought it!

Then I started using MailChimp to advertise my book far and wide, so I didn't just hit them once, I must have hit them about 10–15 times over about four months or so. But during the pre-sales period it must have been at least four to five hits to all my clients, friends, family, acquaintances, people that I didn't even know but were in my database. And people bought it! I was amazed; every day I'd look at my list on PayPal and there'd be another one wanting a book! That was astounding to me. Within two and a half months, before the book was published, I had sold about £1,000 worth.

Another part of the key strategy was a spur of the moment decision of mine. I just thought, 'Wouldn't it be good if people could get from my website a free questionnaire to measure where they are on the spectrum of authentic self versus acquired self?' And so I took the book apart and I pulled out a whole series of strategies which I'd put in the book, then developed them into questions which then produced the questionnaire. So you go on my website, see a free questionnaire which you download, and that gives me an email address to put in my database. I also advertised it on Facebook and LinkedIn, encouraging people to take it and then they could read more about the subject in my book.

When I write and publish my next book, I will use the same strategy and I will be very deliberate about it. I'll tell people very early on that I've got a second book coming and that I've started writing and that I have publishers on board. I'll get people excited about it because I know they respond to that. I will use my database to communicate that and generate some interest. And then as it gets nearer the publication date I will have developed a website for the book and have a PayPal plug-in to pre-order it from the website. And I will then start using a tool like MailChimp to push the book, even when it's still in the pre-publication phase; I will start probably about three months before the book is published to gain interest in pre-orders.

I almost made a mistake. I almost didn't have a pre-sale channel because I didn't have the confidence for it. So that was almost a mistake but luckily became a success factor instead. I thought, even if I don't get pre-sales, I have my own channel for selling the books. And all in all, in the year of publication I probably made about £5,000 worth of book sales just from my website. That's pretty good for a first-time author. Within 18 months I'd sold about 70 per cent of the books and, of those, 25 per cent were pre-sold.

Despite all that, you still need some marketing muscle behind you; you can't do this on your own, especially if you're a first-time author. Chantal Cooke did a lot of advertising and marketing and got me on the radio and all sorts of things. So you can't have that without some marketing muscle behind you. The key thing was to get the book out there and sell it, not to make money from it, and Chantal's services were great because she got me all over the place and I would certainly use them again.

A year from now, you may wish you had started today.

Karen Lamb

Case study 2

A good book, without any PR is a complete waste of time and money.

Vicki Wusche

Case study 2

Vicki Wusche is an experienced property investor and author of three books including *Property for the Next Generation*. Here Vicki explains how her books have helped win more clients, what she did wrong with the first book (in terms of publishing and marketing) and how getting the marketing right with the second book really skyrocketed both the sales of her books and her business…

The first book literally sat in my front room for a month before I worked out how to sell it. I didn't know how to do it, so that's not the way to do it and not something I would recommend to others.

Once I understood more, particularly with the second book, that it's an investment and not just an investment in the time it takes writing the book, but an investment of time to get the book published and get it out there, I started working with Chantal Cooke and we agreed that she would act as my PR for it.

The marketing plan for the second book included a book launch; Chantal worked her magic and did some PR for the event. I also wrote articles under Chantal's guidance that she put out to the press. These articles were designed to talk around the topic of the book and some of its contents and then obviously that would drive people to the actual book.

And then there was also direct selling. Amazon was selling it obviously, but I did direct selling at events and speaking gigs, always carrying a copy of the book with me, and whenever there was a photo opportunity I had the book in my hand or had it somewhere in the room at talks and events.

So the result was that the book, my second book, was published in March 2012 and, with help from the PR generated by Chantal, within 20 months The Telegraph had not only chosen me to be in their launch feature for their property club, but they also listed me as one of the UK's top 25 most influential people in property.

Chantal's PR support and guidance also gained me coverage in The Guardian, Observer, Daily Express, What Mortgage and I was featured by Business Matters. Also, because my third book, Property for the Next Generation, is about preparing your family for a wealthy future, I was then featured in a lot of magazines that families would read. I certainly got a lot of coverage.

I made two mistakes with my first book: not working with a good publisher and not engaging a PR agent from the start.

Having said that there is little point in someone like Chantal publicising a poor book! The book has to be good. You've got to have a good book and you've got to have the promotion to get it out there.

I don't think that's something I could have done on my own: to understand a) the world of publishing and b) the world of journalists.

I can remember a Swiss banker ringing me up one Saturday morning and saying, 'I read about you in The Guardian and The Telegraph and I really want to talk about property with you.' And I don't believe that would have happened with a Tweet or a Facebook post. Those opportunities to share your news are generated by top notch media coverage and that takes top notch and experienced PR.

As a business book becomes older, the sales start to tail off, even if you keep up the marketing. But by bringing out a second book, even though the first book was two years old by then, it still made people go back and buy it. I noticed that one book triggered the sales in another book.

Having written a book, I now attract customers who want to come and work with me; they pay £10,000 to become a mentee or for me to source them a property. So although yes, I get the speaking gigs because of the books, and because of the speaking I sell some of the books in the room, that really is only the tip of the iceberg. The real business sales come from the conversations after the event.

A book leverages your time – it's like a team of sales people. If it's a good book, well-structured with the help of an editor, well written with the help of copy editors and proofreaders, well published and well publicised, then a book can be a top-class sales person for you.

What would you pay to have someone selling for you all the time? Writing a book, even with the cost of the publisher, editor and PR, is still more cost-effective than a member of staff!

My advice to fellow business authors is first understand who it is that you're writing the book for, almost have one person in mind, your avatar. And then also be clear what you want them to do, and of course what you want them to do is to buy whatever product or service it is you're selling.

When you've got that in mind, you have to share that and discuss it with your PR agent. That will help them decide which magazines and the outlets they would recommend that you target. Then your PR agent, if it's a good PR agent, will help you craft articles directed at your target media, to make sure that you have the best chance of getting a published article. You could just write an article and send it out, and maybe journalists would pick it up and maybe they wouldn't.

I wrote articles under Chantal's guidance, she helped with the title, I wrote the content, she helped with the content and when she sent them out, they always got picked up. And, in many cases, the articles got picked up more than once in a month.

Personally, I think a good book, without any PR is a complete waste of time and money. Why write a brilliant book and not tell anyone?

So the only solution is to get your team right; work with a good editor and a good PR agent that preferably both understand what the other is trying to achieve so they help you create not only an excellent book but an excellent marketing strategy to get the book out there to as many people as possible.

Case study 3

The cost of being wrong is less than the cost of doing nothing.

Seth Godin

Case study 3

Chris Arnold is founder and creative partner at Creative Orchestra, and previously a creative director at Saatchi & Saatchi. Here Chris tells us how he successfully marketed his first book, *Ethical Marketing and the New Consumer*, what approaches he used and how (and why) he's already thinking about how he'll market his next book – before it's even written...

I wrote the book in a non-linear way, in other words, you don't have to follow the book chapter by chapter; you can literally drop in and out of the book. This helps with the marketing because it allows me to do abstracts from the book much more effectively; I can take sections out of chapters and publish them. I can give you, say 500–1,000 words from the book that you can publish word for word. So if a journalist is writing an article they might ask me, 'Can you say something about the marketing of renewable energy?' and then I can say, 'Yes, here are 500 words straight from the book', and that makes life much easier for everybody.

To encourage journalists to quote from the book I wrote an enormous list of quotes from it, about a hundred quotes, and sent them out to journalists and said, 'If you're ever writing about these issues, here are five quotes on those issues from the book. Any time you need to, just quote me.' And then I hear about articles where I've been quoted and never even talked to the journalist! But what I've done is I've made their life easier and they appreciate it. And occasionally they would ring me up and say, 'Thank you for that but can I ask you a question?'

I also gave them a close to 24/7 hotline, so basically I told them they could ring me any time apart from between two in the morning and eight in the morning, and I'd get back to them immediately. And you wouldn't believe the number of calls I got on Sunday nights. How many journalists are writing articles on Sunday nights?! So, you make yourself an available expert and in response they are more likely to quote you and your book.

I also kept back one of the chapters, that hadn't been published, and I offered that to a lot of people as an extra bonus to read, and used it as a teaser for the book.

I also considered my target audience. I thought, 'Who are the people most likely to review and write about my book?' So I did promote it to just about every business editor of every magazine and newspaper I could. Then I looked at all the bloggers, and got some really good stuff in America, where a lot of people wrote about the book, in Canada and the US, and even India. Plus I got covered on quite a lot of sites in the UK.

I then utilised the contents of the book and summarised some interesting points and sent those out to people, for example, 'Five things you should never...'. I used this to push the book out to magazines so they had information to complement the book. And that really worked because editorial staff don't have a lot of time today. You know, if you send them a business book, they haven't got the time to read it and write about it. So the more you give them the easier it makes it for them to write.

I also offered books to a number of magazine publishers for free. I did a big thing with the Royal Mail house magazine where they got my books for free and then promoted it in their magazine to 20,000 people. I then sent a lot of stuff to colleges and to tutors on college courses doing marketing, saying, 'This book has been "thoroughly recommended" by xxxx [and I listed some relevant publications and reviewers who had, indeed, thoroughly recommended the book]. Can you recommend my book to your students to read, it's a well written book for students to read all about ethical marketing, friendly marketing and understanding green consumers.' That was quite some work, but led to people starting to put it on course reading lists.

At the end of the day marketing your book is all about the numbers, it's about how many people read your story. You've got to go for the eyeballs, and you've really got to think, 'How many people are really going to see this?' And then you've got to look at how you can engage them because even if somebody sees it, you are only going to get a percentage of them to read it. And then how many are going to be created into customers, how many of them are actually going to want to buy the book? You've got to think it through, you've got to say, 'Who am I targeting, how can I reach them, genuinely reach them, and how can I get them interested enough to buy the book?'

I have started writing my next book, called Thunk, which is about a different way to think. I am analysing a lot of other books about the idea of creative thinking, seeing who's written a good book and who's written a bad book on this, and from there I can work out where the market is. So I'm looking at my next book *from a very marketing savvy point of view. I'm thinking, 'What's my market, how can I best research that market, how shall I write this book so that it best suits this market and maximise the number of people buying it?' So my advice would be, if you have an idea for a book you better look at the market and then tune your book to fit the market because otherwise you're just going to find yourself writing a book for you, not your market.*

Conclusion

Recognize that giveaway items serve as silent ambassadors, reinforcing your Expert Identity – choose them carefully!

Susan Friedmann
author of *Riches in Niches*

Conclusion

Not every tip will work for every author or even every book, but if you are serious about selling your book, then you have to put in some 'legwork' and try as many avenues as possible. Then keep repeating the activities that work for you.

If you've put in all the energy, time and effort to write a great book, then don't keep it hidden – get it out there. A book can really build your business and your profile. But it will only do this if people know about it.

Be sure to track your activity and make a note of what worked and what didn't. Review the strategy you wrote at the start, and the targets you put in place. If you've met your target, congratulate yourself and set some new, bigger ones. If you haven't met them, ask yourself why: were they unrealistic; did you do all the activities you said you would; did you keep track and build on the successes; are there activities you haven't tried yet that would work for your book? Go back to the 'Developing your strategy' chapter at the start of this book and, with your new-found knowledge, rethink and replan your strategy.

Don't give up. It may take time, but your book is worth it.

Use these tips to get your book marketing started, and then use them to inspire yourself to come up with even more ideas to get your book in front of thousands of new readers.

There really is no point writing and publishing a book if you don't leverage it by marketing it well.

As best-selling author Vicki Wusche says, 'A good book, without any PR is a complete waste of time and money' (Interview with Vicki, October, 2015).

Resources

You've written a book that will help people. You therefore have a duty to market it. And keep marketing it.

Chantal Cooke

Resources

I do hope you found this book helpful and feel inspired to promote your business book. To help you make the most of your new-found knowledge, please visit www.TheBookBooster.com/AuthorityBook to download a free checklist of all the tips in this book and an Excel worksheet to help you to plan and track your activity.

You can also download, for free, a 'How to develop your book marketing strategy' document.

Also follow The Book Booster on Twitter and Facebook. Get book marketing tips, publishing news, details of independent bookshops working with authors, new opportunities to promote your book – and much more at:

- @TheBookBooster
- www.facebook.com/TheBookBooster

Extra help

If you'd like more help marketing your book there are a number of ways we can assist:

- Panpathic Communications (www.panpathic.com) – for PR (with guaranteed results) and engaging social media. Whether you'd like us to do it all for you, train you to do it yourself or just coach you in the areas you'd like a bit of extra help – drop us an email. We are always happy to help and have an exploratory, no obligation chat.

  Email book@panpathic.com and we'll schedule in a time for a phone chat. We look forward to hearing from you.

- The Book Booster (www.TheBookBooster.com) – for authors who want to know how to do it themselves. This membership website will teach you everything you need to know to market your book successfully. And if you get stuck or need a little extra help, we're on hand to coach you, answer questions or take over the bits you don't want to do yourself.

  Quote: AG2MYBB code to get an exclusive discount.

- Training – if you'd prefer we can train you (privately or in a group) on how to do all your own PR, how to handle your social media without it taking over your life, other areas related to book marketing, etc. Email book@panpathic.com and we'll call you back for a chat about your needs.

- PR book – *PR Demystified: How to get free publicity by giving journalists what they really need*. This pocket-sized business book teaches you the PR basics for your business. Available from good bookshops and via Amazon.

References

Marketing is a contest for people's
attention.

Seth Godin

References

Buist, W. (2009) *Books Mean Business: At Your Fingertips*, Word4Word.

Wusche, V. (2012) *Property for the Next Generation: Preparing Your Family for a Wealthy Future*, SRA Books.

There is no point putting resources into writing a book and then letting it languish in a box under the stairs.

Chantal Cooke

About the author

No matter what or whom we're talking about, from movies to chiropractors to books to financial planners, the consumer hankers after specialization.

Susan Friedmann
author of *Riches in Niches*

About the author

Chantal Cooke is an award winning journalist, broadcaster and author. She has over 25 years' experience as a columnist for national newspapers and magazines, a broadcast and print journalist, and a radio presenter for the BBC and commercial radio. Chantal has reported from Bosnia and Northern Ireland, and written travel articles for a variety of publications including the *Independent on Sunday*.

In 2002 she set up the UK's first ethical radio station: PASSION for the PLANET. The station, which originally broadcast on DAB and now via the Internet, picked up a number of awards and attracted an audience of over 100,000. During that time Chantal interviewed over 6,000 people.

In 2010 Chantal founded Panpathic Communications and The Book Booster, to use her journalism skills and industry knowledge to help small businesses and authors.

Panpathic Communications is a boutique PR agency specialising in working with small businesses and authors. It offers clients a simple guarantee: coverage every month (or they don't pay for the following month). How can she do this? Because

Chantal understands what journalists want and how to deliver it to them.

The Book Booster is exclusively for authors. This membership website teaches you everything you need to know to market your book and turn it into a bestseller. With in-depth explanations on exactly what to do and how to do it, case studies, interviews with publishers, literary agents, successful authors, journalists, bloggers and so on, plus a section on how to develop your book marketing strategy and a sample strategy for you to follow (or adapt), this website is for all those authors who want to promote their book without breaking the bank.

Chantal is author of the book, *PR Demystified – How to get free publicity by giving journalists what they really need*, has been featured in a number of business books and was even the inspiration for a character in a novel.

Chantal is an experienced presenter and speaker having given keynote speeches at home and abroad, including: IdeasUK (Wales); GoMedia (British Columbia, Canada); Thriller School (California, USA); and many others. She also regularly delivers social media training at the Foreign and Commonwealth Office and the British Council, and her PR training clients include The RSPB, Fujitsu Siemens and BT.

Chantal is passionate about helping business authors promote their books. She believes that as authors we have a duty to get our books out to as many people as possible in order to share our expertise and experience. By sharing knowledge, everyone benefits.

You can contact Chantal via email: book@panpathic.com

Follow Chantal on Twitter:

- @ChantalCooke
- @PRDemystified (for PR tips and press coverage)
- @TheBookBooster (for book marketing tips and news)
- @PASSIONftPLANET

LinkedIn:

- www.linkedin.com/in/chantalcooke

Facebook:

- www.facebook.com/TheBookBooster
- www.facebook.com/PanpathicCommunications
- www.facebook.com/PassionForThePlanet

Websites:

- www.TheBookBooster.com
- www.panpathic.com
- www.passionfortheplanet.com

Also by Authority Guides

The Authority Guide to Financial Forecasting for SMEs: Pain-free financials for finance and planning
Simon Thompson

Build a better, faster forecast.

In this Authority Guide, forecasting guru Simon Thompson shows you how to build financial forecasts quickly, effectively and cheaply through his unique, proven and easy-to-follow 10-step process. By learning how to create effective forecasts you will master the ability to understand the potential financial outcomes for your business and be able to communicate financial information in order to successfully raise investment or loans.

The Authority Guide to Emotional Resilience in Business: Strategies to manage stress and weather storms in the workplace

Robin Hills

How do your challenges inside and outside of work impact upon your emotions and your resilience?

The emotional resilience of those involved in a business will contribute significantly to the organisation's success. This Authority Guide from leading emotional intelligence expert, Robin Hills, will help you change the way you think about yourself and the way you approach potentially difficult situations. You will be able to develop your own personal resilience and understand how to develop resilience within the hearts and minds of your team and your organisation.